take
me
back

Copy Editor: Emily Soli

Book Design by Nuno Moreira, NM DESIGN

ISBN (Paperback): 979-8-9924364-0-2

ISBN (Hardback): 979-8-9924364-1-9

ISBN (Ebook): 979-8-9924364-2-6

POEMS ON HEARTBREAK, HEALING,
AND SELF-DISCOVERY

take
me
back

amanda rodriguez

To my fiancé, Adam, who is my greatest love,
best friend, and biggest supporter

TABLE OF CONTENTS

PART 1: TOXIC LOVE

SILENCE

Silence speaks louder than words
But you don't hear me when I'm quiet
You're not in tune with my emotional response
You're not listening to my silence

My lack of words is to gather my thoughts
It doesn't mean I am being compliant
I practice thinking before I speak
Don't assume I am weak when I am silent

Our disconnect has become severe
Communication is where we're reliant
If you choose to disregard my honest words
At least pay attention to my silence

MUSE

Your art is to abuse
Skillfully, you emotionally confuse
Your true colors are a changing hue
Tell me, am I your muse?

Do I inspire this abuse?
Why am I your canvas to bruise?
A masterpiece to lose
Only painting me with blues

Romanticism misused
Only seeing the artist's point of view
Trying to piece together the clues
Tell me, am I your muse?

BROKEN DISHES

Breaking dishes
Fighting in the kitchen
I never imagined
We'd be in this position

Blacked out in my mission
To call your attention
By breaking dishes
Could I get you to listen?

To force your submission
To notice me crying in this kitchen
It's your love that I'm missing
You're in an emotional remission

Burning bridges
Going against my intuition
Losing my inhibition
Spiraling in my suspicions

You manhandled me to listen
Shocked and unsure if it was malicious
Now we're in this hurtful position
Numb, and standing over broken dishes

MEAN IT

If you're done with me, mean it
Don't leave me confused

If you love me, mean it
Don't let that word go misused

When you promise me, mean it
Don't make my heart feel abused

When you apologize, mean it
Don't leave our relationship bruised

When you comfort me, mean it
Don't feel obliged or unenthused

When you walk away, mean it
Don't pretend you have something to prove

If you're over us, mean it
Don't reach out to feel amused

If you want to work on yourself, mean it
Take some space to get back to you

If you wish me well, mean it
Because I only want the same for you

When you decide to love yourself, mean it
So your heart can be renewed

WANDERING EYE

It happens when you're drunk or high
The not-so-subtle stares as other women pass by
It's like an urge you have to satisfy
A regular bad habit, I call it your wandering eye

I question whether you're trying to be sly
You're so obvious, and I'm right by your side
You chalk it up to "just being a guy"
You have no idea the insecurities it magnifies

Time after time
That wandering eye
Your attempts to feel justified
Causing my aggression to intensify

Our arguments amplify
No control over the way I reply
In secret, it makes me cry
And when I blow up, I'm vilified

It's something you don't deny
You say you'll work on it and have nothing to hide
But the message is already implied
And my self-esteem needs to be rectified

TRAUMA BOND

Even after all you've put me through
Being together feels familiar and calm
I don't know why I go back to you
It must be a trauma bond

My desire for you goes up and down
Even more when we're at odds
You'll poke me to ignite my fuel
Because you know I will respond

We're back and forth, our fights won't stop
I need a break from what's going on
Five minutes after our intense fights
We're embracing, in each other's arms

We're high, then low, then spiraling
An ongoing cycle of abuse we've caused
The only reward I'm seeking from you
Is to help me break this trauma bond

COMPROMISE

Please, can we compromise?
I'll meet you halfway
I'll stand by your side
But I need you to stand by mine and stay

I just need you to compromise
Don't let your ego get in the way
I'll give you what you want
If you keep your manipulations at bay

My desire is not to win
Your partnership is what I crave
Things are not always black and white
Let's work together and stop placing blame

It can't always be what you want
My feelings should matter too
When you stonewall, it shows me
That you're only thinking of you

Please, can we compromise?
This relationship I can't lose
Don't take advantage of my heart
Don't give me an ultimatum to choose

RIDE OR CRY

I'm either with you or without you
Your ride or cry
Your way or the highway
Get out or comply

Accept this baggage or you'll take flight
Your ego has come to a mass
Leave me to sit in coach
Go upgrade your seat to first-class

This is who you are
You're either in or you're out
No compromise within your character
I am left with or without

This is not what I signed up for
I don't want to be your ride or cry
I don't want to be your victim
I just want to say goodbye

NAKED

You always say you love me naked
But naked is all you can see
You love my skin, my hair, my silhouette
You only love my physicality

You never truly see me naked
You know nothing beyond skin-deep
You're blind to who I really am
So undetermined to know all of me

My fears, my dreams, my passions
My vulnerabilities
Unrecognizable when you strip me down
I'm a stranger emotionally

Beautifully raw and fully exposed
To bare my depth in totality
You lack the ability to break down my walls
You don't know me at full capacity

I stand here naked, fully clothed
My entire presence in full visibility
But the naked truth is you've never loved me
You can't love what you're unable to see

STAY

Give me a reason to stay
Don't put your ultimatums on replay
Your manipulation causes me to obey
It's just easier to resolve it this way

Emotionally, I am your prey
My self-respect is starting to decay
But without you, I'm too afraid
Conditioning forces me to stay

"I love you" is what you can say
Reassure me, and I'll forgive you today
Why do I give and continue to pay?
I have no reason to want to stay

ANGER

Anger in my heart
And fear in my soul
You get me to the point
That I lose all control

I fight to my core
I fight to the death
I fight until I win
I fight until my last breath

You bring me to tears
You let me unfold
After it's all over
I'm numb and I'm cold

I live for your love
But your love makes me cry
The further apart we become
I get too angry to try

You say I've given up
But what else can I do?
My motivation is crippled
And I can never guess your mood

My needs go unheard
I repeat them again and again
When you refuse to compromise
The blood rushes to my head

My aggression takes over
And I start seeing red
I black out in frustration
And don't realize what I've said

I've never felt this before
The 0-to-100 that I range
Something rushes over me
And I can't keep myself contained

Are you the victim? Who knows
I'm the one who feels abused
The emotional trauma that I suffer
Your targeted chaos has me confused

Anger gets the best of me
When I'm pushed to my limit
So you aggravate my aggression
And your fighting defenses pivot

You make me think I'm crazy
You leave me with so much self-doubt
You say such hurtful things to me
And then chastise me when I shout

Your silent treatments spark hysteria
You ignore me day and night
And when I cry to break the silence
You hit me with guilt trips and gaslights

You say I'm too emotional
I feel talked down to and judged
I beg for us to work together
But you avoid blame and won't budge

We've been here before
I've experienced this course
I have nothing left to give
This isn't something I want to force

So yes, I hold anger
For loving you in vain
I need you out of my life
So I can be happy again

EYE CONTACT

Look me in the eyes when you lie to me
Let your eyes tell me what you're thinking of
Let your eyes show me honesty
I know your "truth" is a version you made up

A cowardly stare leaves you exposed
Your eyes tell what you're too afraid to say
From the first time you said "I love you"
To the last time you said you couldn't stay

In the moments we lock eyes
My emotions are paralyzed
Disappointment in the form of cries
I see beyond what you try to disguise

Look at where this gets us
I'm seeing clearly and not looking back
Visualizing a better life ahead
All from your eye contact

BODY IMAGE

My reflection in the mirror
Observing what I see
Mentally picking and poking
Judging my imperfect body

Absorbing and accepting
Trying to keep a positive mentality
It's hard *not* to be critical
Under a feminine beauty ideology

You were the one I turned to
To lovingly encourage me
To motivate and remind me
That you accepted me for me

It hurt my self-image
When you compared them to me
Those unnatural, full-figured women
Women who clearly had plastic surgery

That can never be me
I cannot help my anatomy
But you made me feel guilty
I wasn't what you wanted me to be

Discussions back and forth
On what "we" thought I'd need
A larger chest was your answer
It would fit me perfectly

Your enthusiasm was triggering
You even offered to cover the fee
You looked me in my eyes
And said, "Do it for me"

Flashbacks in my mind
Of the girls you'd constantly seek
The way you stared at them
Was not the way you stared at me

Satisfying your desire
I knew wouldn't make me happy
I didn't want to change
But I wanted to feel sexy

I was emotionally conflicted
And trapped in self-grief
Unconsciously unaware
That you didn't love me for me

I needed to escape you
You were the demise of my self-esteem
The only body change I needed
Was keeping *your* body away from me

Body image is a mental construct
I can't let opinions influence me
Taking power over my perception
Allows me to love myself confidently

This beautiful body of mine
A vessel that affords me clarity
The improvements to be made
Are improvements internally

My inner self is evolving
It's flourishing constantly
Who I see and cherish in my reflection
Is ultimately up to me

INTUITION

I should have trusted my intuition
It warned me from the beginning
As my emotions continued spinning
My common sense went missing

I put myself in this position
Chasing a life I was fictionally living
Caught up in illusions and misgivings
My unconscious mind was winning

I should have listened to my intuition
A unique gift bestowed on women
It was guiding me toward a better decision
But my heart wouldn't listen

ONLY SO MUCH

There's only so much
One person can take
It's exceedingly impressive
The amount of chaos you create

Confused by your affection
Torn between love and hate
What I suffered with you
Was the most painful to date

One day, I was adored
The next, your inmate
Feeling abused and ignored
Every conversation was a debate

Confronted by your lies
Secrets you couldn't keep straight
Defaulting to the silent treatment
Refusing to communicate

You blamed me for fighting
And wanting to separate
While you disappeared for hours
With no concern to explain

You positioned me as an outcast
Used family and friends to triangulate
You attacked my insecurities
Causing my neediness to accelerate

Grand efforts to make me jealous
Using other women as bait
Fully aware of my distress
You were testing what I'd tolerate

Concerned you'd crossed a line
Attempting to comfort my emotional state
Reassuring me of your affection
Rewarding me with the love we'd make

You'd finally apologize
To defuse all the hate
I fell for your manipulation
Causing your ego to inflate

The good days were rare
Your mood was hard to navigate
As if your true self had depleted
And needed my tears to rehydrate

I found the strength to leave
There was only so much I could take
Two weeks later, you called me crying
Claiming that I was your soulmate

Still vulnerable to your love
And in a delicate emotional state
You took advantage of my weakness
I took you back and did not hesitate

You promised me the world
All the effort you would dedicate
I believed in you this time
You moved in, we couldn't wait

As time went by
Reality started to resonate
The relationship became abusive
Resentment began to cumulate

I was no longer your interest
We were no longer intimate
Some nights you wouldn't come home
I felt insecure and inadequate

We were back to where we started
Finding it impossible to communicate
I tried compromising to make you happy
You wouldn't budge unless you got your way

You completely checked out
Took every opportunity to alienate
You were no longer my lover
Now you were just a roommate

I hoped that things would get better
But this suffering I couldn't escape
It was time to put myself first
It was time to finally separate

I was scared to be alone
But it was the right decision to make
I knew that I deserved better
There's only so much one person can take

CRIMINAL

You hijacked my heart
Just like a criminal
You stole years from my life
Our love was fictional

I thought I was your home
You made me feel irresistible
No one robs an empty house
My fulfillment made you miserable

The more I had to give
The more I felt invisible
I couldn't read your signs
Your communication was subliminal

Masterminding my devotion
What you gave back was conditional
Like a thief, you ran me dry
Your manipulation was cynical

Your plan was well designed
What you took from me was pivotal
I was a victim of your crime
I was taken by a criminal

WHAT YOU WANTED

I tried to make you happy
Tried to give you what you wanted
I shut my mouth
I played the part
After a time, I was exhausted

Your demands became unfair
You didn't care about what I wanted
You didn't budge
You pushed me away
You were checked out and coldhearted

I tried to make it work
This isn't what I wanted
I couldn't change your mind
Even when I changed myself
Your persistence couldn't be halted

You left me all alone
Our relationship is now haunted
You made your bed
You reap what you sow
You got exactly what you wanted

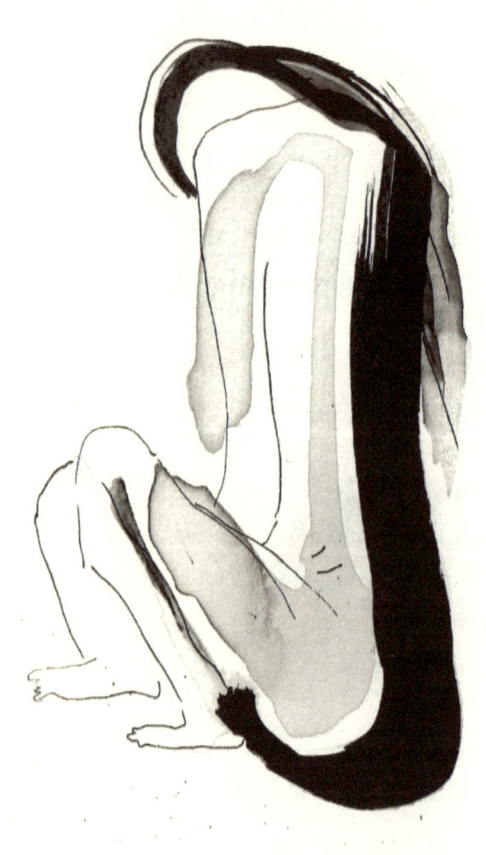

PART 2: ALONE

ON MY OWN

Here I am
All on my own
Gutted and lonely
Left with no home

You broke my heart
Away you went
Dismissed my love
And the years we'd spent

Boxes and tape
Leaving behind memories of hate
A new future I'll create
Your apologies are too little, too late

I'll cry today
But tomorrow I won't
I'll come out of this stronger
Because I did it all on my own

MY LOVE HAS CHANGED

How can it be real love
If the love has changed?
I feel enraged
I feel so estranged

You no longer see me
I am not the girl you claim
We're no longer a team
What was it that changed?

Our connection is different
Your demeanor is not the same
Your heart feels so numb
My emotions are rearranged

My love, you're distant
You're out of range
My heart is broken
Now my love has changed

I feel so shortchanged
For this unfair exchange
You disappeared, unexplained
And left me emotionally strained

Lost in feelings of shame
Nothing left but remains
Without you feels strange
But we needed this change

FOOL

You fooled me once
And schooled me twice
Our relationship was a gamble
But I rolled the dice

A second chance at love
And I paid the price
I wanted us forever
You were my heart's only vice

We jumped in too fast
Our love became cruel
We only got along
If I played by your rules

But I learned my lesson
Like an adolescent in school
I only got played
Because I was the fool

WHY I DRINK

When I'm with or without you
I need a drink
I'm forming a bad habit
I use to not think

Like a stone thrown in water
I quickly start to sink
I drown my sorrows
With every sip I drink

While living together
We fell out of sync
I had no idea how to fix it
And my emotions came to the brink

Sitting alone on my couch
Treating my glass as a shrink
I'd go to bed numb
So I didn't have to think

I felt lonely with you
Then you were gone in a blink
So many glasses in a day
I found comfort in each clink

With every bottle I finished
It caused me to think
My attachment to alcohol
Started with you as a common link

I LIED

Our relationship
I couldn't take it
At times
I lied

Secrets you kept from me
I couldn't face them
To myself
I lied

My love
You wouldn't claim it
To my heart
I lied

My trust
You would break it
In public
I lied

So unhappy
I couldn't escape it
I was living
A lie

Emotionally detached
I would fake it
In bed
I lied

I was optimistic
We could make it
To you
I lied

The truth
I couldn't say it
I'm sorry
I lied

NOSEBLEED

I've always been so serene
Never suffered from anxiety
But after a year of my relationship
I started having nosebleeds

It happened when we would fight
Tensions high or he was ignoring me
I didn't think much of it
But it was my body warning me

Telling me to breathe
To relax my anxiety
To not ignore my internal needs
My body was helping me to see

Red flags running from my nose
It was the message that I'd need
To finally pay attention
To what my relationship was doing to me

My relationship was changing me
And drops of blood were calling my attention
Oblivious to what was going on
It was my body's way of forming an intervention

Self-medicating my stress
A drug and alcohol technique
All of this was just a phase
We'll be back on track next week

While masking my reality
My nose continued to bleed
Triggering my motivation
To escape this self-induced misery

I knew what I had to do
And I knew where it would lead
But I was still in love with him
And couldn't find the strength in me to leave

Overwhelmed with apprehension
My head and heart disagreed
Thankfully, he beat me to the punch
He said his love had changed for me

The strength I lacked to leave him
Was no longer something I'd need
He let me off the hook
He did a favor for me

In hindsight, I'm incredibly thankful
We were simply not meant to be
He released me from our toxic relationship
And since then, not one nosebleed

ERASE MY LOVE

Erase my love

Don't chase my love

You wasted my love

You hurt me, love

You changed your love

You grew out of love

You left me lonely, love

Give me back my love

I can't be without love

I need your love

Can't breathe without your love

Was this really love?

How could you leave me, love?

How could you destroy this love?

Why did I believe in this love?

In you, I found my love

But then I lost my love

It was an angry love

I fell in love

I fell for love

I was tricked by love

I was crippled by love

Erase my love
I won't chase you, love
You broke my love
I can't forgive you, my love
Be gone, my love
I can't keep you, my love
Because this is not love
And I deserve a real love

MISTAKE

Your pattern of misguided love
Brought tears to my face
A 360 experience of suffering
And here I am, alone at your wake

To pay my respects
To say my goodbyes
To honor our past
To leave the pain I survived

Take with you the lessons we learned
From this devastating heartbreak
Losing me is best for us both
But loving me was your biggest mistake

Never again will you experience my joy
My compassion or my sensual touch
The way I comforted you in the darkest times
How I supported you as an emotional crutch

Never again will I make you laugh
Or secretly kiss you while you're sleeping
The way I'd stare into your eyes with trust
And put your hand over my heart to feel it beating

Never again will I call you mine
Or give you my heart, body, and soul
Never again will you get the pieces of me
That you always said made you feel whole

My depth of love and commitment to you
Will be a bond that's hard to replace
I've set a high bar few women will reach
Which is why loving me was your biggest mistake

PROBLEM

I can finally breathe now that you're out of my life
Everything with you seemed to be a problem
Your job, your friends, your family drama
Always complaining, but no intention to solve it

Comparing yourself to everyone else
Never satisfied, whining and solemn
It was draining for me to carry your confidence
You weren't aware of how bad it had gotten

It was hard to be happy when you're so up and down
Emotions changing like leaves in autumn
Life's easier now that you're no longer mine
Now you're someone else's problem

DISTANCE

Attachment and love
Can be confusing in appearance

Manipulation and anger
Disabled our coexistence

Control and desire
Incrementally fed into our persistence

Codependency and passion
Were the only things that felt consistent

Partnership and compromise
Where our hearts met with indifference

You versus me
You chose yourself in an instant

The pain from the past
Now feels hauntingly reminiscent

The good and the bad
I'll never regret what had existed

My heart versus my brain
Self-love is my ultimate commitment

Know that I will always love you
But only from a distance

EMPTY SPACE

Several weeks have gone by
I've been alone in this empty space
The walls are missing your artwork
Your things are no longer in their place

I sit on my couch and look to my right
I no longer see your face
In bed, I try to center my body
To avoid feeling your empty space

Cooking for one no longer calms me down
I used to cook and you'd wash the plates
Loss of appetite while pain eats me alive
Crying here in this empty space

Coming home and no one is here
Your arms unavailable for my embrace
I grab a drink to calm my nerves
My means of comfort has been replaced

I paint the walls and rearrange my things
So your memory has no trace
Trying my best to rebuild this home
So I can fill the void in this empty space

Sometimes I sit alone in silence
Wondering what the future awaits
Praying to finally find real love
And move on from this empty place

I KNOW I HURT YOU

I know that I hurt you
I knew what my words would ignite
A poorly used defense mechanism
And I used it every time we'd fight

I knew exactly how to hurt you
There's no excuse to validate I was right
I wanted to hurt you the way you hurt me
I was acting out of spite

I hurt you because I was hurting
A vicious side of me came to light
I would blow up and verbally abuse you
To feed my aggressive appetite

I want to apologize for hurting you
I realize my words carry a lot of weight
Regardless of the pain I felt
I should have handled it better in hindsight

RAGE

Forgive me for the things I said
Forgive me for my rage
I'm regretful for all the time I spent
Focusing on the hate

I chipped away at your patience
Your self-esteem was frayed
I lost control, I lost myself
My emotions took center stage

I became verbally abusive
And still you chose to stay
My inner demon wanted out
Like a barbaric animal in its cage

Life is tough, and I assumed
That this was just a phase
But now I know I needed help
And our relationship was to pay

I'm haunted by the damage done
I blame myself that you disengaged
I'm ashamed for all the strain I caused
And now we are estranged

That's not the way to express myself
The uncontrollable anger I displayed
Forgive me for the things I did
And said when I was enraged

I've gotten help, I promise you
I'm on my way to permanent change
It does not erase what I put you through
No one deserves that type of interchange

I'm breaking bad habits and forming new ones
You'd be proud of the progress I've made
I'm putting in the work I need
I've finally turned a new page

Looking back on us as I heal
I feel it's important for me to say
Losing you was the lesson I needed
You inspired my coming-of-age

I HAVE YOUR SWEATPANTS

I keep your sweatpants in my drawer
But I don't wear them
I can't bring myself to throw them away

I found your toothbrush in the trash
It used to sit next to mine
I cry; I'm not OK

You left your hot sauce in the fridge
I barely use it
But I might today

The empty left side of my bed
Remembers the times
We slept in all day

Empty picture frames around the room
I'm mourning a loss
Our love is no longer on display

An overwhelming silence fills the room
I'm thinking of you
It feels like you passed away

Your presence still lingers within these walls
I sage the space often
But it manages to stay

I can't keep living my days like this
Trapped in anxiety
I need to let go of this heartbreak

It's finally time to get over you
I need to accept it
And be on my way

Although it hurts to think of you
I'm moving on
And I know, one day, I'll be OK

I COULDN'T FIX YOU

Have you changed, or is it still you?
I'm mad, but I still miss you
You're no good, but I can't dismiss you
To love me, I could never convince you

Compromise was the issue
Putting us first didn't fit you
Control is what conflicts you
Your command, I would not submit to

A conversation I want to give you
But if I see you, I might forgive you
It's irresponsible for me to be with you
I can't let this toxic cycle continue

The lessons learned ring true
Good luck is all I'll wish you
And hope one day it hits you
You're the only one who can fix you

GHOST

The energy still lingers
All the negativity we provoked
Replaying our arguments in my head
It feels like I'm fighting with your ghost

Crying at the top of my lungs
Alone with no one to host
Sobbing from the love I recently lost
It feels like I'm calling to your ghost

At night, I can't sleep
In bed is when I miss you the most
Staring at the space you used to fill
It feels like I'm lying next to your ghost

I take a pill to numb the pain
I can only function when I'm slightly dosed
I need relief from this reality
It's my way of repressing your ghost

This affliction is too overwhelming
I write down the emotions it evokes
Words therapeutically pour out of me
It's like I'm talking to your ghost

As time continues to pass
I read back the memories that I wrote
The heaviness starts to disappear
I'm finally releasing your ghost

Your energy no longer lingers
My positivity has been invoked
Writing you out of my life is therapy
It's what the universe diagnosed

ANXIETY

I am a victim of my mind in society
Thoughts and feelings quickly turn to anxiety
Trying to rid this rush that's inside of me
Internalizing the struggle to maintain my privacy

Overwhelmed, it feels like I'm spiraling
Disengaged, I feel like I'm losing me
Stop and think about what could be bothering me
Breathing deeply as my chest starts tightening

Reexamining my stress in its entirety
Refusing to give in to what's overwhelming me
What's out of my control won't support my vitality
Mental health is my number-one priority

STARING AT THE CEILING

When can I see your face again?
When will I escape this feeling?
Some days, I can't get out of bed
I just lie there, staring at the ceiling

Paralyzed with grief
Wondering if this is how you're feeling
Why haven't you reached out to me?
Is this your process for healing?

My loneliness is revealing
I'm completely broken from you leaving
An unhealthy way of dealing
Just me, my thoughts, and this ceiling

I LEFT THE LIGHTS ON

I left the lights on at night
Hoping you'd find your way home
Would you drive past my place and see them on?
Would you think of me and reach for your phone?

Sleeping with no clothes on
Vulnerable and crying all alone
How long until this pain is gone?
All this pain I carry on my own

I left the lights on every night
But you never made it home
I'm scared I'll never be near you again
I'm afraid of the unknown

My intrusive thoughts shine in the light
I have to stop myself from reaching for my phone
I know there's nothing left for me to do
Because you've already moved on; you're gone

WAITING

Thinking of you
I reached out to you tonight
Feeling weak
My head and heart still collide

Having hope
Praying I don't get denied
Sitting patiently
Still waiting on your reply

Meditating
So much anxiety I feel inside
Second thoughts
Will I be left satisfied?

Feeling foolish
I gave him the power to decide
Reminiscing
I thought our love would last a lifetime

Impatiently waiting
He still hasn't replied
Keeping busy
I move around to pass the time

Judging myself
It's too late to change my mind
. . . Left on read
Feels like he took away my air supply

I NEED TO LET YOU GO

I know I need to let you go
Because my heart deserves to heal
The hurtful things we've said and done
Were painful and difficult, but real

I know I need to let you go
This grieving process has gone too far
Close the wound that cut me deep
Leaving me with a scar

I find myself still loving you
Even though I know it's wrong
Confusion as I mourn this loss
What we had was just a con

The heavy pain is so real and intense
It reminds me of what we had
I think of you almost every day
My heart, it breaks; I'm so sad

I miss your touch, your kiss, your aroma
I hear you in every love song
I know I need to let you go
Take the first steps toward moving on

My love for me is stronger than
The grief I'm holding on to still
I promised myself I'd let you go
And let you go I will

AMNESIA

In my moments of weakness
My moments of amnesia
I forget how much I suffered
I only remember how much I need you

I'm in a battle with myself
Heart and mind in the same arena
I lose sight of what's right for me
I fall victim to being a Libra

I want to have you close
But I separated from you for a reason
I can't lose my memory
I can't allow abuse amnesia

SUNSETS

You love a good sunset
You love the purples in the sky
When the sun finally set on our love
Seeing those purples only made me cry

Looking at the horizon
I wonder if you're looking too
Cotton-candy colors fill the sky
Each beautiful sunset makes me think of you

I look forward to the night
When it's dark, I look for stars
Finding light in the evening gloom
Each twinkle brings healing to my heart

The sun may have set
But it brings the renewal of sunrise
The dead of night was my survival
In daylight, I'll come back alive

I MISS

I miss your tender chest
Being my headrest
Listening to your heartbeat
In love and feeling blessed

Holding you tight
When my mind was at rest
Feeling safe with you
And emotionally caressed

I miss your sweet words
Your love language expressed
The guitar songs you played
When your love was professed

The overwhelming feeling of passion
It was hard to digest
I miss loving you
Instead of feeling depressed

PART 3: RELAPSE

TAKE ME BACK

Take me back
To the day we met
I wish I could turn back time

Not to cause change
Or a butterfly effect
But to tell myself, "It'll be all right"

Take me back
To the girl I was
So I can prepare her for what's to come

Warn her that the man she loves
Is not what he seems
And there's a lot in her path to overcome

Take me back
To that first painful night
Which ignited my prolonged suspicion

On that night
I want to tell myself
To never go against my intuition

Take me back
So I can hold her hand
And comfort her as she cries

I want to promise her
She's going to make it through
And she'll come out stronger on the other side

Take me back
To the day we met
So I can look him in his eyes

Assure him with confidence
The suffering he'll put me through
Will be a blessing in disguise

WHY COULDN'T IT HAVE BEEN ME?

Why couldn't it have been me?
The girl I changed myself to be
To fit the standard I thought you wanted
A girl who wasn't me

I wanted us to work it out
Instead of staying, you chose to flee
I said, "I'll change; don't leave me, babe"
But you clearly didn't agree

You put yourself above our love
You chose her over me
And here I am, beside myself
And now we'll never see

What could have happened if we tried?
Were we truly meant to be?
I cried myself to sleep at night
No longer caught up in a dream

For months on end, I thought of you
I'd lie awake in your debris
Through the fighting and hurt, I learned a lot
I earned a broken-heart degree

I sit at home and wonder, love
Why couldn't it have been me?
I see you moving on with her
So quickly after me

It's not your fault for moving on
This is the best thing that could be
Now I can rebuild and start fresh
Without this heartbreak blinding me

I don't want anything from you
I am no longer holding grief
Instead of wondering, "Why couldn't it have been me?"
I'm choosing to be free

ROUTINE

Do you take them to the same old restaurants you took me?
Do you play them the same playlist that you kept on repeat?
Do they sit through the same shows you watched on TV?
Are they accommodating to your lifestyle? Do they fall into
    your routine?

Do you judge them on appearance, as if they need to compete?
Do you show them off in public because it boosts your self-esteem?
Do you ignore them when they speak, while you're busy
    scrolling through IG?
Do you give them the same treatment you always gave me?

Has anything changed
Other than you being with me?
Do you still suffer from your fragile male ego?
Do you still thrive in consistency?

Your spirit has no depth
Your predictability is a well-oiled machine
I was simply a placeholder in your lifestyle
Your lack of substance couldn't be seen

You're completely unaware of yourself
Unaware of anyone else's needs
One of the worst parts about having been with you
Is knowing I was only part of your routine

BAD DAY

Do you ever have days
When you think of your ghost?
Your mind can't stop wandering
Wondering about the one who hurt you the most

Thoughts that consume you
Reliving moments in resentment
Feeling confused by your pain
But knowing it's better to accept it

Your anxiety starts to peak
You're frustrated with your mind
You just want to forget it all
Leave that hurt and fear behind

You're mad at the truth
And the thought of them makes you sad
You waste an entire day
Spiraling about the life you once had

Your productivity falls short
You're unmotivated and distracted
You're caught in a mental game
You're emotionally held captive

Why do they get to move on?
Are you the only one who's hurting?
Why are these feelings still lingering?
What's left for you to still be learning?

All day turns to all night
Your spirit is left in dismay
Get some rest; tomorrow will be better
We'll just call this a bad day

GOOD MAN

After months of healing from you
A man who left me traumatized
You randomly called me late one night
It took me by surprise

Triggered by your phone number
My body was paralyzed
What were you calling about?
What made you call tonight?

I thought I had moved on
Yet this was a scenario I'd fantasized
Your regretful call was what I wanted
A manifestation of my cries

My curiosity got the best of me
I knew answering was unwise
I took a risk to hear you out
Even if it led to my demise

Your voice stirred mixed emotions
But none I could verbalize
You said you were checking in on me
But I knew it was a lie

You were lost in a lonely world
Your "concern" was all a disguise
Turns out the life you were leading
I had incorrectly glamorized

True to form with your persuasive game
I had no reason to sympathize
From the desperation in your voice
I could tell you were compromised

Your intention was not to make amends
Not to check in or even apologize
Your intention was to feed your ego
Leaving my emotions antagonized

This was simply a sorry attempt
To reconnect and harmonize
In a single breath, you said you missed me
And were in a relationship that coincides

A poor excuse for a man
And with this new girl, I could only empathize
I felt blessed to know I'd escaped from you
All your selfishness and self-absorbed lies

I pray one day you'll grow up
See your faults and moralize
If not, you'll continue to radiate pain
From the trauma you internalize

Thank you for reaching out
Calling to "check in" was quite a surprise
I was most thankful to see who you really are
You're no longer a good man in my eyes

I DIDN'T FORGET

Just because you want to come back
Doesn't mean I've forgotten how you left
I forgave you for the pain you caused
But your actions had a lasting effect

You left me alone to fend for myself
Now you're here, sobbing with regret
You now have to learn to stand on your own
You need to solely deal with the unrest

I survived the past and now thrive in peace
Your presence in my life, I no longer accept
You're the man who left me broken, abandoned, and weak
And that's something I'll never forget

UNHAPPY

Are you unhappy in your relationship?
What is it that you need?
Did you find the grass isn't much greener?
Is that why you keep reaching out to me?

Is it attention that you're seeking?
Or do you want to play her like you did me?
You're making that poor girl look stupid
And you're boosting my self-esteem

Please send your girl my sympathy
Because that dumb girl used to be me
Luckily, I was able to survive you
I hope she figures out that you lie and cheat

I hope she catches you in the act
I hope you expose your true identity
A man like you doesn't deserve honest love
You deserve to be alone with your own misery

Every time you reach out to me
I look down on you with pity
You don't love yourself, you're not content
And you'll always be unhappy

REGRETFUL

I know you feel regretful
That our relationship came to a close
From the way you're running back to me
I can tell I loved you the most

Fake boobs, long hair, full lips
She's the type you always chose
You replaced me with the kind of girl
Who only knows how to smile and pose

All these years as a fuckboy
Your misogynistic glorification is exposed
Isn't this what you wanted?
Why are you unfulfilled by this girl you chose?

I see you finally realized
That losing me was a major blow
I'm sure by now you've noticed
Your inability to grow

The longer you were with me
The more your confidence rose
Now you're watching my progression
While yours has halted and froze

You miss having me in your life
You miss the way our connection flowed
You miss the way I loved you
You miss the confidence I bestowed

You see me with a new glow
Embodying my sexuality like a pro
You see me moving on
It's time for you to let me go

I see you checking on my status
I feel you holding on to hope
No need to tell me you feel regretful
Trust me, I already know

BOUNDARIES

You had your chance to love him
You gave it up in eight years' time
Why does your ghost still linger?
Please let him go now that he's mine

This is not a competition
But his focus should be on me
I need you to keep your distance
Please bow out respectfully

When you frequent through his mind
I worry he'll be led astray
He feels a need to protect you
To feel confident that you're OK

I acknowledge what you both shared
Your past, I would never downplay
Can I trust your "good intentions"?
Or is this an attempt for you to stay?

It pains me to have concerns
What I question, I cannot trust
Maybe you hold my best interests
Proving my relationship is unjust

Maybe I misjudged you
You know him better than me
Maybe you want to expose him
So I can see past what I believe

I should consider you an ally
Not feel guarded or attacked
Your presence brings me clarity
I'm ready to take my power back

You gave me true perspective
Uncovered intuitions I should not ignore
You're more than welcome to shoot your shot
You can have him if he loves you more

HELLO AGAIN

I hadn't thought of you in months
Finally felt like I was in recovery
Until I saw your message
Asking how I was and if we could meet

Looking at your text with nothing but pity
Laughing out loud because . . . finally
Classic men, when they eventually see
How unflattering life is without me

I was overwhelmed with curiosity
And my ego got the best of me
Walking toward you so confidently
I was relieved to feel no animosity

I knew what was happening
You were flirting and touching all over me
We immediately had sex; it was grappling
We both relapsed after our recovery

It was nice to be with you
It was comforting
From the couch to the bed
We were cuddling

Like no time had gone by
We enjoyed some drinks
We lay there, catching up
Fully reminiscing and in sync

Another round—we had too much to drink
You stood up and smiled with sincerity
Looked right in my eyes and admitted to me
The multiple times you'd cheated on me

Shocked and confused while I'm listening
As far as I knew, you were faithful to me
An overwhelming pain came over me
Our years together were no longer a reality

I couldn't understand your reasoning
It felt like you'd said it with intentions to hurt me
I put on my clothes with a racing heartbeat
Back on my path toward recovery

You had no idea what the truth meant to me
A cruel low blow from your blunt honesty
I sat at home, ruminating on this discovery
I needed time to digest your adultery

I felt deceived and disrespected
Beyond angry
I was losing my mind
My ignored intuitions became concrete

This is the type of shit
That'll make a girl go crazy
This is the type of man
Who will strip her of emotional safety

I thought I was healed
I thought it'd be harmless to meet
But I took a major step back
That was a mistake I won't repeat

FEEL BETTER

Do you feel better?
Now that you got that off your chest
To admit you'd been cheating on me
Is your conscience put to rest?

We broke up almost a year ago
Why choose now to tell the truth?
I think you just wanted to hurt me
Because you see me doing better than you

You could have kept it a secret
But felt it was important that I knew
The girl you're currently dating
You met while I was still dating you

She might have been the last
But she certainly wasn't the first
You said it had gone on from the start
Your infidelity was never coerced

You said it was better that I knew
So I could "hate you and move on"
Convincing yourself you did me a favor
Your ego has gone above and beyond

Now do you feel better?
Do you feel more like a man?
Cheating on your girl and confessing your truth
Was this all part of your plan?

Thank you for opening my eyes
Clearly, my love blinded me from the start
But hearing how much you disrespected me
Reopened wounds still left in my heart

Maybe I needed that final letdown
To see how you hurt people for pleasure
You were right; I hate you and can finally move on
I hope that makes you feel better

LIAR

You assured me that my suspicions were wrong
You convinced me I was your only desire
You promised you would never hurt me
You're simply a talented liar

Talentless in love
Talentless in honesty
Talentless in dignity
Although I knew that subconsciously

You said you lied for my own good
To shield me from the truth withheld
If you thought lying was going to protect me
You were only lying to your fucking self

Truth be told
It was the truth you couldn't hold
Time allowed the real you to unfold
You are a liar, exposed

THEY ALL KNEW

Secrets brewed
And they all knew
Your family
Your friends
All covering for you

They all knew your secret
And I was the fool
Fool me once
Fool me twice
They all witnessed what you put me through

I trust it's what they're used to
Your secrets are like déjà vu
It's a character flaw in you
And now their character, I devalue

Now I know the truth
I understand their point of view
Their loyalty lies with you
Their disrespect, I can't undo

The secrets grew
And they all knew
They hid them from me
To save you
So I cut them out of my life
At the same time I did you

MY SUSPICION

Lost in my intuition that you'd been unfaithful to me
Up at night contemplating what I didn't want to believe
My mind racing with thoughts of you and infidelity
My suspicious heart ached, wishing you'd come clean

I lost my feminine power to a man who didn't deserve me
The anxiety and self-doubt still burn fresh in my memory
All I ever asked from you was respect and honesty
My suspicions of you had completely taken over me

Thank you for manning up and finally coming clean
For the unfaithful nights you came home and lay in bed next to me
My reservations about you are now confirmed and put at ease
You are released from my life so I can move on in peace

THE OTHER WOMAN

The other woman
Is who I came to be
For the man that I lost
I lost my identity

I'm angry with myself
For diving in so carelessly
And to you, the other woman
I want to say I'm so sorry

I know how it feels
To fall victim to infidelity
And this man we both know
Left us wounded narcissistically

If you're clueless to what's gone on
I take accountability
I hope one day you read this
And accept it as my apology

The trauma this man carries
Spreads like a virus unintentionally
I truly believe he has no idea
How poisonous he's come to be

He played with both of our hearts
While playing house with you and your baby
When you were blissfully unaware
He was also sleeping with me

This is not my reality
This is not who I choose to be
I respect you as a fellow woman
I respect you as a strong mommy

You never deserved this treatment
And I take responsibility
This is not the message I want to send to the world
And I'm ashamed for breaking our femininity

Trust that you'll never have to worry about me
I've accepted he's not a man I need
I pray that he tells you and chooses honesty
He has no validation or right to ever cheat

To all the other women
The unknown count he has allowed to intervene
I hope this man helps us grow emotionally
Because the other woman is not who we want to be

DISHONESTY

Your dishonesty got the best of me
I was unable to see
The love I shared unconditionally
You didn't deserve it; you were unworthy

Does she know when you're lonely
You miss me in secrecy?
Does she know when you're not around
You're calling my phone repeatedly?

Have you shown her who you are?
Who is it that she sees?
When will you reveal your true identity?
When will she know you're a man incomplete?

I can't help but send her sympathy
What you're doing to her, you already did to me
How many women were there ultimately?
How many of us did you destroy emotionally?

I believed you were a man of quality
I gave you my heart and showed loyalty
I honored your character so foolishly
I trusted your love and dishonesty

NOW I CAN SEE

Now I finally see
The cunning tricks you played on me
All the lies you led me to believe
All the ways you managed to cheat

Now I finally see
How you lie about where you'll be
Not mentioning who you'll meet
Why you clutch your phone so securely

Now I finally see
Because the cheater now is me
I'm the one you're planning to see
While she's home alone with her baby

Now I finally see
Just how easy it is to cheat
Just how unfazed you seem to be
This is part of your personality

Now I finally see
This is the man you'll always be
I was another veteran in your fleet
My love you never deserved to keep

Now I finally see
How manipulative you can be
How you thrive on codependency
How unhappy you'll always be

Now I finally see
Just how damaged I seem to be
How I fell out of recovery
All the guilt I now carry with me

I'M NO BETTER

I'm no better than you for what I've done
I broke a commitment to myself
And just like you
I broke her heart
I was lustfully compelled

I know better than to do this to her
I relapsed from my breakup pain
The same pain I suffered
I enabled for you
I look down on myself in such disdain

I know better than to reward your lies
I know it was wrong to entertain you
I had a weak moment
I disrespected myself
Even after what I'd already been through

There's no better way to explain myself
Than to say it to her face
But just like you
I choose to cover it up
I choose to take it to my grave

I know better than to do what I did
I'm ashamed of the woman I had become
I was selfish and weak
I know the universe will punish me
I'm no better than you for what I've done

AGAIN

Here we go again
You're more consistent than paying rent
Every first of the month, you're texting me
Asking if you can see me again

I don't care about how you've been
Or that your relationship has come to an end
It's time you lose my number
For yourself you need to fend

My kindness is not an open door
Please don't mistake us for being friends
I forgave you as a favor to myself
So I could detox and emotionally cleanse

You're not a presence I want in my life
Your character I cannot defend
I'm shocked you still hold on to us
You were never good to me; let's not pretend

You no longer exist to me
That's something you need to comprehend
I've asked you repeatedly to stay out of my life
Don't make me say it again

SELF-HELP

You may have cheated on me
But you only cheated yourself
Take our history together
And place it on your bookshelf

To reference the memories of a virtuous girl
Who leads a beautiful life full of wealth
Take my story and use it for good
Use my chapter for your own self-help

WHAT IF IT WERE YOUR DAUGHTER?

What if your daughter were cheated on?
What would you say?

What if you found out she had been lied to for years?
Would you encourage her to stay?

What if you knew she was being manipulated?
Would you look at her the same way?

What if he left her but kept crawling back?
Would you do anything to keep him away?

What if your daughter were emotionally abused?
Would you tell her how a real man should behave?

What if a man treated your daughter how you treated me?
Would you think it was OK?

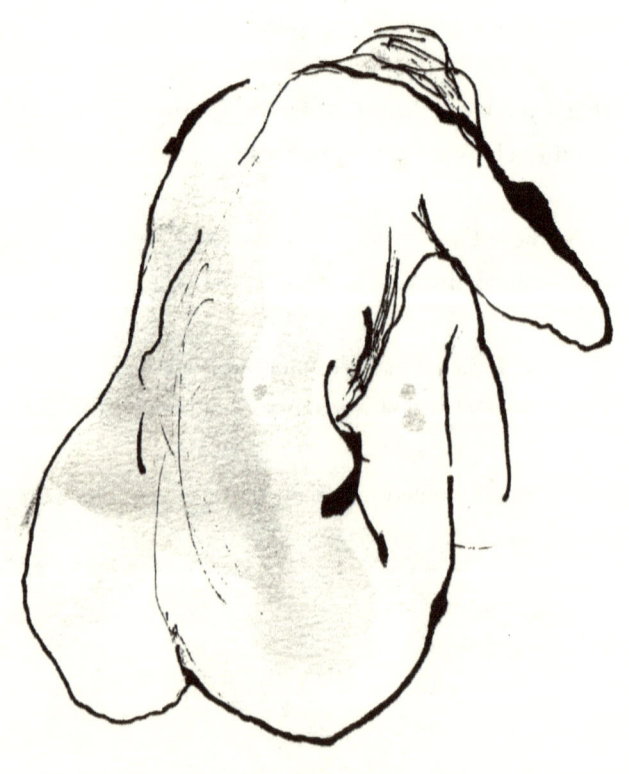

PART 4: RESENTMENT

RUTHLESS

Your intentions were ruthless
And I was beyond clueless
You were living a double life
Everything we had, simply fruitless

Now you're stuck here feeling useless
Because I no longer choose us
Your jaw dropped, now you're shocked
Covering your mouth like you're toothless

Your seed is now rootless
You're unsettled by my aloofness
I finally took back my power
I'll show you what it means to be ruthless

PERFECT CRIME

You played me for a fool
It was the perfect crime
You got all my love, trust, and loyalty
So you could lie, cheat, and steal my time

I was blinded from the start
My trust is given until it's taken
I gave you all of me
But it was too late before I was awakened

You got away with murder
Because a piece of me died
But you inspired my resurrection
And now your regret will coincide

I've discovered my own purpose
And you were a pawn for my gain
My intentions to you were true
Serendipity would better explain

I know that you feel the shift
Our auras have been left on display
I'm levitating while you're standing still
Karma for you still has debts to pay

You planned the perfect crime
Unaware of the future it would hold
Your future is led by your design
Ultimately, it's all in your control

WHO ARE YOU?

You're not the man I thought you were
I just needed more time to tell
But you turned out to be a helpful man
Because you released me from this hell

There's still a boy inside of you
Will he grow up? Only time will tell
I promise that when you figure it out
It'll hit you like a bombshell

You're not the man I thought you were
You're a lonely man with an empty well
You sucked me dry of my energy
You left me drained, alone, and unwell

This is the man you'll always be
Your track record is how to tell
You're everything I'll never want
And I'm thankful we said farewell

MISTREATED

Are you aware of the pain you inflicted on me?
Will you apologize for the way you tormented me?
To what degree do you truly believe
That I deserved to be treated like emotionless property?

The words you'd speak
The way you'd insult me
You led me to believe
You were the best I could achieve

Passive-aggressively
You knew exactly how to trigger me
Unaware of how well you read me
Your manipulation went unperceived

Was it entertainment you'd seek?
Picking fights and ignoring me
Or was it attention you needed
After I suspected that you'd cheated?

You called me crazy
You threatened to leave
It wasn't until we were done
I had dry eyes and could finally see

It was your insecurity
Your low self-esteem
Your nonexistent masculinity
Your overwhelming self-pity

You are a man incomplete
And that caused you to bully me
I was captured in your deceit
But at last, I've been released

I will no longer be deceived
To be away from you, I am relieved
It took some time, but I finally see
I'm so much greater than what you allowed me to believe

CRAZY

If all of your exes were "crazy"
Then maybe it wasn't just me
Maybe you weren't the victim
Maybe you caused some hostility

It's easy to call a girl crazy
To attack her emotionally
Placing blame and putting her down
Escaping accountability

If all of your exes were "crazy"
Why did I choose to be so naive?
I didn't factor that you were the constant
Or question your accusations' consistency

There are two people in a relationship
True love is not always guaranteed
I never imagined I'd fall for your trap
I'd be another girl you'd mistreat

With all the men I've dated
I've never had this much difficulty
With you was the first time I felt it
A recurring sense of unease

Ignorant because love is blind
I couldn't see the red flags right in front of me
I never considered what might happen
If we broke up—what you'd say about me

If this is your accusation by default
It would be easy to only blame me
It'd mean I'm just like the rest of them
And you'd take no responsibility

If all of your exes were "crazy"
I assume that's how you'll portray me
I won't allow it ever to faze me
People can believe what they want to believe

What if you're the one who is "crazy"
And it was something I chose not to see?
Maybe you're the one who's unhealthy
Maybe it's you and not me

FACE

Like attracts like
Are you prepared for the karma you'll soon face?
Because what goes around comes around
Your destructive breadcrumb trail has been traced

The universe never forgets
Your false self will be defaced
You'll get a full dose of your own medicine
What you've gotten until now was just a taste

When it's time to pay your dues
Be mindful of the people you've disgraced
Center yourself and ask for forgiveness
So your negative karma can be absolved and erased

There are good and bad in the world
Where will you choose to take your place?
After karma hits, you'll need to make a choice
Will you continue to live in this toxic space?

You can change your broken path
Your bad karma can be replaced
But first, you need to deal with your past
The poison you caused, you'll eventually face

BEST-CASE SCENARIO

Best-case scenario is that you've moved on
I hope you found all that you need
Best-case scenario is that you're finally happy
So you no longer need to reach out to me

Best-case scenario is that I know all the facts
I know you lied and cheated on me
Best-case scenario is choosing to forgive you
Even though I know you're not sorry

Best-case scenario is that I accept who you are
A toxic man who takes no accountability
Best-case scenario is that you stay away
You're the worst type of man I could meet

Best-case scenario is that I find safety in my own arms
I wasn't safe with the man meant to protect me
Best-case scenario is that I take this as a lesson
And figure out the qualities in a man that I need

Best-case scenario is that I rely on myself
I'm the only one who can take care of me
Best-case scenario is that I put myself first
With you, I was never a priority

Best-case scenario is a life without you
I need to be rid of your toxicity
Best-case scenario is I let go of the past
So I hold no resentment and move on happily

FIGHT OR FLIGHT

I'm terrified of running into you
Because I'm uncertain of what I'll do
Seeing your face after all this time
Triggered by what I suffered through

If I ever saw you again
The best version of me would stay calm
Ignore your presence, disregard your existence
A subtle way to cause your ego harm

The best version of me is not the only version
A part of me would want to act in spite
Expose you as a treacherous man
Bring all your foul, dirty laundry to light

I'd step to you so we're eye to eye
Introduce you to the new me
Size you up and down in pure disgust
Smirk at you and exit casually

I expect to never see you again
It's unfortunate we live in the same city
To be honest, it's a moment I've worried about
And if it happens, I hope you'll ignore me

Do not try to acknowledge me
Do not try to stand in my line of sight
I can't predict my organic reaction
With you, it'll be fight or flight

All this time away from you
I have not prepared myself to see you again
I pray it never has to happen
So I can bring this anxiety to an end

KICKING THE CAN DOWN THE ROAD

Are you taking time to heal
Or just kicking the can down the road?
Inward action creates change
Otherwise, it's the same show, new episode

Diving into a new relationship
When your life comes to a crossroads
Means you depend on others to make you happy
Avoiding self-awareness will cause you to implode

You need to deal with your traumas
Take time to be alone
Look within to uncover your truth
Be vulnerable to the insecurities you'll decode

Healing takes work
It can become an emotional overload
But the personal gain is worth it
Instead of kicking the can down the road

NO WORDS

I had no words to say
My silence was not consent
You put your hands on me inappropriately
With malicious sexual intent

I had no words to say
I was in shock as I looked at you
What I thought would be a reactive scream or slap
Ended up being silence as I withdrew

I wasn't prepared for this
No one coached me on what to do
Treading water in uncharted seas
Drowning in confusion as I came to

You violated my peace
Made me feel guilty from your pursuit
You devalued my discomfort
You claimed my accusations were untrue

Falsifying what happened
A smear campaign I can't undo
It was my word against yours
The audience you built behind you grew

I crumbled in the spotlight
The only way to win was to lose
I revoked my strength as a powerful woman
Feeling ashamed that I couldn't push through

I had no words to say
But there was so much that I learned
The experience altered my point of view
And since, my feminine confidence has been affirmed

As women, we have a voice
We have a responsibility to uphold
We cannot stay silent when we're victimized
Or we give these degenerates the control

To the man who disrespected me
The man who left me with no words
Our next encounter will not be a silent one
And that should be the least of your concern

MEN LIKE YOU

What is it about me
That attracts broken men like you?
The time we shared was a setback
Clearly, my sensibility withdrew

I had already learned my lesson
But failed the assignment when it came to you
I played with fire, and I got burnt
Knowing exactly what I was getting into

Luckily, I've been conditioned
I've learned to self-soothe in solitude
Nothing you do could hurt me
No more than what I've already been through

It was a sting to my ego
But the only hurt one here is you
You're a charmer and a snake
Who holds no personal value

You use people as a Band-Aid
To avoid uncovering the darkness within you
Your personal development is a fraud
Because your only concern is you

You're a trigger to my conscience
Despicable men like you
You remind me of what I survived
And what I never want to go back to

TOXIC TRAIT

Why do I always go for the wrong guy?
Is this my toxic trait?
You'd think I would've learned by now
But I consistently take the bait

I try to see the best in them
But I'm only sealing my own fate
Broken men cause broken hearts
This cycle of abuse, I need to escape

At first, they're the perfect guy
I'm love-bombed, and we isolate
By the time I start to see red flags
My heart's invested, and it's too late

I change myself to make them happy
I learn to acclimate
With time, it gets exhausting
And being my true self becomes a debate

I lose myself to secure our love
Relationship pressure and I bear the weight
I find myself in familiar territory
Up and down, feelings of love and hate

It's time to end the rotation
Of the broken men I choose to date
Build awareness and take accountability
It's time that I self-educate

There is power in learning your faults
Finding solutions to navigate
The best part about loving the wrong men
Is that it exposed one of my toxic traits

FUCKBOY

He was so handsome and charming
Like a playful new toy
But my triggered alarms were ringing
I knew he was a fuckboy

So flirtatious and confident
But with no good intent
He was the exact type of man
I've learned to resent

He didn't know my past
Had no idea what he was up against
You can't win a losing battle
And I won't entertain that content

I politely disappeared
Afterward, he never entered my mind
Feeling proud that I'd learned my lesson
I didn't fall for the fuckboy this time

There are weeds in every garden
With time, you'll know to pluck them out
If not, the universe will keep testing you
Until you finally figure it out

UNTAMED

I'm a self-proclaimed man-eater
You're but a means to an end
The time I choose to spend with you
Has no lasting intent

My emotional wall is up
What you offer is fun and play
I take pride in the art of seduction
I take my time as I conquer my prey

Empowered by sexuality
Inspired by the thought of love
Guarded from my painful past
Liberated by what I rose above

I have no desire to find a partner
I'm still healing from the damage
Just looking to get my feet wet
My intentions are purely savage

Your role is to fill a need
When I snap my fingers, run to me
I'll devour you with my sexuality
And when I'm done, I expect you to leave

As I grow into this alter ego
I'm thriving in my power
As my confidence continues to peak
Your masculinity starts to cower

I guess I'm into role-play now
Because I've just flipped the script
My dominance elevates your desire for me
While also leaving you to feel less equipped

A power move in female form
I'm the hunter who now provides
The sexual control I have over you
This untamed woman has your hands tied

SETTLE

Once the dust settled
I finally settled the score
I tried to settle down with you
But I knew I deserved more

Never again will I compromise my worth
Or allow your manipulative nature to meddle
Never again will I rationalize my feelings
Never again will I fucking settle

I have rectified my soul
Persevered in what I've been through
I've never been the type to settle for less
I have no idea why I ever settled for you

COMING TO TERMS

Coming to terms
On my own terms
I had a lot to learn
I had a lot to unlearn

My respect you never earned
My love you never returned
My life has taken a new turn
My life is no longer your concern

LOVE

Wrong-from-the-start love
Head-under-heart love
Not-being-smart love
Better off apart, love
Bleeding-heart love
Torn-apart love
Toxic-counterpart love
Need a restart, love
Ambitiously embarked love
Faded-spark love
Left-its-mark love
Left-in-the-dark love
Ripped-from-my-heart love
Played the part, love
Negative-remark love
Thankful to depart, love
Now I can restart love
Lessons-for-the-heart love
Lead-me-toward-my-art love
Blessed we are apart, love

LISTEN TO YOUR BODY

Sometimes I stay home alone
Closed off from the world
It's the only way I feel safe
When my emotions go unheard

Life can be overwhelming
My path to clarity can start to blur
When I listen to my body
I pay close attention to emotions submerged

Being mindful of life's stressors
Allows my peace of mind to go undisturbed
Taking a break from the outside world
Is a habit I was forced to learn

I need to check in with my conscience
So my energy can be preserved
I take this time to be grateful
For my experiences and all I've learned

The good, the bad, and the hurtful
All lead to the blessings I have earned
Sometimes I stay home alone
To let my body know it's being heard

I SURRENDER

I surrender to my emotions
It's the only way I can heal
I surrender to the unconscious mind
I surrender to what my body needs to feel

I embrace the pain to release this corrosion
Simply "letting go" is not enough to make it real
I surrender to my emotions
My soul has come to kneel

I allow the mind and spirit to remain open
I now absorb all that is real
My chemistry needs to stay in motion
So my new truth can be revealed

TIME

Your time is coming, my dear
You will be rewarded for facing your fears
You've survived the difficult years
Your prayers did not fall on deaf ears

Your manifestations are near
Your good fortune will appear
The universe is about to shift gears
Everything will soon become clear

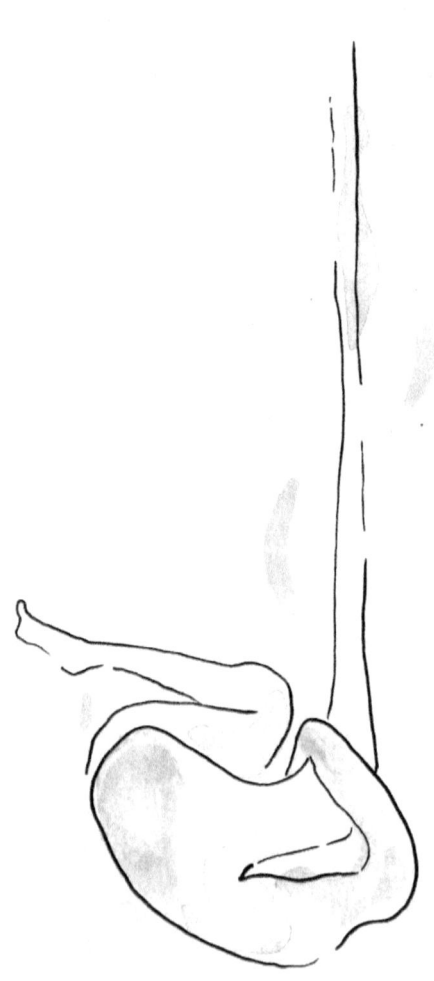

PART 5: HEALING

PHASE

I was the sun that gave you light
My brilliance went ablaze
You were my moon, and true to form
Your emotional presence went into a phase

From light to dark, your illumination faded
As you turned away, your gravity pulled me in
Your force of attraction was powerful yet dark
It burned my light and it turned me dim

Time would pass; you'd cycle a phase
Your love was full, then it was gone
I couldn't keep up
    Did you love me . . . ?
        Want to leave me . . . ?
            . . . Were you hiding a liaison?

The stars aligned so the truth could unfold
My light is shining toward better days
I've been released from your pull
I've come back to earth
    Your time in my life
        Was just a phase

PREY

I was prey to you
A malleable girl to choose
A manipulated inmate to use
Someone you consistently pursued

Your game was quick to confuse
But you were someone I trusted at root
Weaponizing my kindness for abuse
I was your prey to hunt and seduce

Today, I'll pray for you
Because I finally see your truth
I pass my forgiveness on to you
I pray to heal this emotional bruise

I will not let this lesson go misused
Your behavior I will never excuse
I carry this scar because of you
I hope my prayers find their way to you

MIRROR

Every day, I look in the mirror
And I love what I see
Which is why I fell in love with you
You were simply mirroring me

My likes and dislikes
You mirrored my personality
You tried to become my reflection
But you were just deceiving me

Uncertain of who you are
So you copied my identity
You play the part of the hero
When your true character is the enemy

I fell in love with someone
Who I actually thought completed me
But it was all smoke and mirrors
The real you only cheated me

Seven years of bad luck
A broken mirror to our trilogy
Our superficial love was a superstition
Your misfortune will serve you, undoubtedly

Now, when I look at you
I'm no longer impressed by what I see
You no longer have me as a mirror
And you'll never measure up to me

Today, I look at myself in the mirror
I still love what I see
I'm confident, I'm beautiful, I'm independent
It's no wonder you mirrored me

FIGHTER

Distance has made my heart much wiser
You are no longer whom I desire
Your company no longer serves me
You are not the kind of person I admire

Loving myself and knowing when to quit
Are qualities I've finally acquired
I've released the suffering that trapped me in the dark
That moment of my life has been retired

The tough times pushed me to be better
To grow and feel inspired
My soul has finally found peace in your absence
And my emotions have been rewired

I am grateful for the time we shared
Because the challenges made me wiser
Now I understand who's worthy of my heart
My standards have been set much higher

As I reflect on the past and turn toward the new
My future only looks brighter
By continuing to protect and honor my strength
I am choosing to be a fighter

PAINFUL PEACE

My growth has come
From a painful peace
Hurt builds character
I've awoken my inner beast

Inspired by personal progress
Undistracted by a false reality
Navigating this painful peace
Rediscovering love in totality

A unique transformation
This pain has caused me
I'm dynamic in disposition
I'm flowing with creativity

Through pain, I've uncovered peace
I've discovered a new version of me
I was forced to grow from pain
And become the strong woman I was meant to be

SPEAK

Ladies
Don't crumble like me
If a man puts his hands on you
It's important that you speak

Speak your truth
Speak you mind
Become aware of your boundaries
Don't feel pressured to lie

Tell someone immediately
Make an example of every man
Regardless of how minor it may be
We'll never find justice unless we stand

Stand together
We believe you
Don't feel intimidated
This is our moment of #MeToo

No man is entitled to our bodies
If we don't speak, they'll never learn
Call them out on their violating actions
Their respect for women should be earned

My biggest regret is not speaking up
These men I trusted put their hands on me
To avoid tension, I kept my mouth shut
For their comfort, I ignored my own boundaries

I wish I would have said something
In their disgusting moments of power
Turned the tables to make them feel ashamed
Exposing them as true cowards

As women, we all have a voice
And discomfort can make us feel weak
But together, we can end our silence
As women, it's important that we speak

YOU SAVED ME

You saved me from a life I never had to live
You saved me from a love I knew you couldn't give
You saved me from the inner pain that I often hid
You saved me from believing what I knew I couldn't admit

You saved me from forcing something that simply didn't fit
You saved me from the fights that I wasn't able to predict
You saved me from the exhaustion of convincing you not to quit
You saved me from holding on to a toxic relationship

You saved me from unhappiness, and now I'm happier within
You saved me from sleeplessness, and now the glow has come
    back to my skin
You saved me from doubting myself, and now my life's the best
    it's ever been
You saved me from resentment, and now I'm finally ready
    to forgive

I FORGIVE YOU

I forgive you for the nights when you were weak
I forgive you for the lies that never ceased
I forgive you for the betrayal when you'd cheat
I forgive you for the nights you left me crying in our sheets

I forgive you for the times you'd emotionally retreat
I forgive you for the promises you'd never keep
I forgive you for loving me the least
I forgive you for bringing me to defeat

I forgive you for constantly criticizing my body
I forgive you for making me doubt my self-esteem
I forgive you for never extending apologies
I forgive you for not being the man I needed you to be

I forgive you for the traumatic fights that brought me grief
I forgive you for making me think you were in love with me
I forgive you for hiding the emptiness you felt underneath
I forgive you for being a man who is incomplete

I forgive you so I can finally release
Release the energy of a love that broke my peace
I forgive you so my heart can be at ease
So I can accept the new blessings coming to me

ALONE

I've experienced a lot on my own
But it never meant that I was alone
The support I needed was a phone call away
Solitude is the reason I've grown

I've hugged myself at night
I've cried myself to sleep
Practiced affirmations in the mirror
Even when my confidence was only skin-deep

It took mental focus and discipline
To finally feel emotionally safe
Breaking chains from the toxic attachment
That I thought would send me to my grave

At times, I didn't know if I'd make it
It's unnatural to live in quarantine
This broken girl with a broken heart
Mended the shattered pieces into a dream

I've pulled myself out of the darkest days
I take pride in the strength I've shown
Transformed my life all by myself
But that doesn't mean I was ever alone

STARTING OVER

It's never easy
To overcome heartbreak
Stress and self-doubt
Can be challenging to navigate

Facing your traumas
Allowing self-reflection to resonate
Can be the missing piece you need
To accept the past and reevaluate

Humans can be draining
Their negativity can intoxicate
Take it as a blessing in disguise
Choose yourself and separate

Who is the person you want to be?
What is the passion you strive to emulate?
You now have the power to start over
Take the opportunity to rebuild and recreate

Every step forward
Is another chance to self-motivate
You'll set out on a path
Where you can truly trust and elevate

Move on from the past
You must lead and liberate
Take ownership of your story
The one you choose to narrate

GOOD ENERGY

I missed you lying next to me
I missed your cologne scent on my sheets
But missing you and wishing you were here
Is no longer serving me

I sage my space to rid my mind
Of your lingering energy
I'm letting go of your memory
Because my sanity I need to keep

My heart, once shattered, now is whole
And I'm finally at peace
I'm letting go of resentment and pain
I'm forgiving your deceit

I thank you for our experiences
What I learned and what you taught me
I'm grateful for the impact you left
Thankful for the wrong way you loved me

Finally, I can let you go
Your presence I no longer need
Now I see that falling out of love
Was a path leading back to me

I've set the bar for what I deserve
My standards I will uphold and appease
You've inspired a transformational year
My new life is becoming a masterpiece

I feel the universe rewarding me
With motivation to succeed
To rise above and restart my life
The negativity needed to cease

Without you here, I can find real love
The kind that's meant to be
I deserve the same energy that I gave you
The good energy I release

SPIRIT GUIDE

It's been months since our love has died
It's been weeks since the last time I cried
I still think about you all the time
Not a day passes when you aren't on my mind

How long until my emotions subside?
I thought I'd sorted what I was feeling inside
A force pulling my thoughts to your side
I feel the reason is something divine

My heavy heart wants to leave you behind
But thoughts of you spark my creativity inside
You motivated me to open my mind
I started writing about the love we survived

My passion for words is no longer confined
The heartbreak I carried can finally be set aside
I trust there was a reason you were put into my life
I believe the universe assigned you as a spirit guide

WE BOTH WON

We were never meant to be together
The way we loved each other was wrong
That doesn't make us bad partners or bad people
But our relationship was a bad one

Individually, we're better off
We should be thankful that it's done
Now we get to find a healthy love
So, separately, we both won

DREAM

I see you in my dreams
Why does your phantom follow me?
Are you thinking of me in your sleep?
You send me vibrations when you are weak

I can feel you missing me
When I dream is when we speak
Reconciliation is what you seek
But I can't forgive what you did to me

I hope your heart finds release
So we can end this nocturnal therapy
To forget you is my dream
May your memory rest in peace

PEACE OF MIND

The stars aligned
The way my life was designed
I believe in the divine
And my struggles were well timed

I had to lose my mind
To find my peace of mind
To stay on my mental grind
Not allow myself to fall behind

With my emotions intertwined
I was surprised to find
I was no longer confined
A new version of me was revived

I embrace all that is mine
My spirit is one of a kind
I'm blessed that I could find
A constant peace of mind

BREATHE

As you breathe into your awakened self
Breathe power into your dreams
Breathe life into dormant parts of yourself
Resurrect the good that lies beneath

Calm the mind and reset your soul
Just remember to breathe
Inhale the divine through your nose
Exhale positivity through your teeth

With every breath, manifest your future
With every breath, center your soul
With every breath, believe in yourself
With every breath, feel yourself becoming whole

MANIFEST

Manifestation is key
You cannot become what you can't see
I will not marginalize my successful future
I will take control of what's in store for me

I'm an instrument of the divine
A higher power is guiding me
Through meditation and self-awareness
I've been rewarded with mindful opportunity

I'm focused on living with intent
So I can conquer my dreams
Visualizing what I want
Has the power to serve me what I see

Trust in this power
You can manifest anything you believe
Learn to understand your unconscious mind
And your mental state will become reality

TAKING CARE OF ME

Sometimes I surprise myself with the woman I've come to be
So often, I've faced hard times and fallen victim to adversity
I've always managed to claw myself from the dark to find
    prosperity
And the hard lessons I suffered through gave me
    awareness and clarity

In the darkness, I've grown emotionally
In the light, I've built myself mentally
Through it all, I've embodied my creativity

Reflecting on what I've acquired, everything I gave to me
I did it on my own, and I'm proud of myself
I'm happily taking care of me

10/10/2020

Why are you following me?
What does it mean?
I keep seeing repeating numbers
What is the universe telling me?

My intuition will not fail me
I have to stay focused, trust myself, and believe
This divine influence through numbers
Has a purpose it wants me to see

Mindful of my vibrations
I'm making good choices to benefit me
As I'm healing, in recovery
These signs put me at ease

I've been manifesting a positive year
Of good luck and complete inner peace
I read these numbers as guiding lights
Confirming my path toward growth, left unseen

I trust that this is my year
I can't escape all the signs I see
My heart is open to allow positive change
Bringing transformation and serenity

GUARDIAN ANGEL

All connections carry a purpose
You have to be aware of what life brings
Is it possible that I was your guardian angel
And you chose to rip me from my wings?

I believe we all have a reason to meet
Maybe our reason was to uncover flaws
Maybe our love was bigger than us
And we were together to break down each other's walls

Our love was so complicated
But from despair comes great strength
I trust the universe had us meet for a purpose
To learn how to take real love to great lengths

It's hard to understand why you were placed in my path
Would God allow me to suffer this much pain?
In the end, I understand we were never meant to last
We were brought together because we had lessons to gain

With you, I uncovered many truths
Discovered traumas I didn't know existed
In a way, our relationship was like therapy
And I finally faced the demons I'd resisted

I trust I was a light in your life
Put in your path to help you grow as a man
But my presence could only take you so far
Our growth together outgrew its wingspan

I'm proud of who you were toward the end
Although you hurt me, I could see a major change
Not regarding infidelity or self-confidence
But your motivated presence that took the stage

We set each other on positive paths
To be better humans, although it was painful
Our experience generated an internal awakening
Maybe we were each other's guardian angels

REFLECTION

I chose to love you and all of your imperfections
I chose to reflect what I wanted to receive
I chose to give you my trust, love, and affection
But the way you loved back was not a reflection of me

I forgive myself when I look at my reflection
I forgive myself for what I couldn't see
I forgive the way I was bullied with rejection
That's not the type of girl I choose to be

I trust my growth and spiritual resurrection
I trust that, in love, it will soon be my turn
I trust the reciprocation of my positive reflection
Because what I give out is what I'll get in return

THANKFUL

I'm thankful for our experience together
I'm better because of you
Your betrayal toward me was a blessing
You're responsible for my spiritual breakthrough

I'm thankful for the love you gave me
Although your love was untrue
I'm now able to distinguish a false self
I learned to recognize that from you

I'm thankful for all the arguments we had
They gave me a new point of view
I've seen the results when you don't fight fair
I now know that some things you can't undo

I'm thankful for the bond we had
And how quickly you withdrew
You opened my eyes to your character flaws
I saw a side of you I never knew

I'm thankful for the pain I felt
You left your mark like a tattoo
It reminds me of the inner strength I gained
And the self-confidence I needed to renew

I'm thankful for the motivation you inspired
I'm taking charge of my dreams coming true
With you, my mind was unproductive and unfocused
Now I have a clear vision of what I want to pursue

I'm thankful to have had you in my life
You forced my self-discovery, and my powers grew
I'm thankful for the woman I've become
I'm better because of you

PART 6: SELF-LOVE

THE NEW ME

Hello to the new me
The girl I wished I'd be
The girl you never met
The girl who's finally free

Free from pain
Free from anxiety
Free to love again
I'm making myself a priority

Hello to the new me
I'm healthier mentally
I'm focusing on myself
I'm gaining clarity

Clarity on the past
Clarity in my maturity
Clarity in my path
Toward the new and better me

I AM RESILIENT

I was stripped of my mental and emotional wealth
I forgot who I was and needed guidance to help
I lost all expectations for my life and myself
I was unprepared to experience the cards I'd been dealt

I devalued my potential and the standards I'd upheld
I put others' needs above mine; self-love was withheld
I let negative habits lead me to self-destruct and rebel
I was stuck in an unhappy thought pattern as if cast under a spell

I had to change my mindset and make an effort to get well
I was irresponsible to lose myself over the emotions I felt
I reached out for support to break through my internal shell
I was honest with myself and ready to bid my heartbreak farewell

I finally regained confidence, and my empowerment excelled
I noticed a positive change in my overall health
I'm proud of the growth that I built within myself
I am happy again and will let my resilience speak for itself

THE VIKING

You came into my life with perfect timing
For a year, the electricity we were awkwardly hiding
We saw each other weekly; our sexual energy was striking
My relationship was on and off but steadily declining

We felt the connection between us quickly rising
An escape from my heartbreak you were providing
Letting go of the inhibitions I was intentionally fighting
You swept in and raided my body, just like a Viking

Your long curly hair, Adonis body, all enticing
Kissing, touching, pulling, sweating, biting
The chills I felt when our bodies were uniting
All-consuming, the way our attraction was abiding

The universe planned on our souls coinciding
We were two troubled hearts, both of us were finding
The law of attraction, I felt it arising
Did divine intervention cause our intertwining?

Our future was grey; I never thought about what might be
But I felt at my core that our timing was aligning
Healing each other from the pain we were both surviving
All the while, our sexual connection was igniting

I never questioned our bond or what it might mean
Our relationship was a moment in time but so exciting
You were put in my life for a reason, with perfect timing
I'll always be thankful for you—my warrior, my Viking

SEXUAL PEAKS

Subtle effort but full body
Your sensuality makes me scream
How you tease me and slightly choke me
I'm living my own wet dream

Pushing your weight against me
We're rhythmic like a team
Arching my back while you soothe my skin
So effortlessly, I cream

Resting your head on top of my chest
Giving me a second to breathe
Pressing your lips to my collarbone
This sensory overload has me in disbelief

Sliding my body to the edge of the bed
Your stamina has never known defeat
You kiss me and rest your forehead on mine
My legs tremble as you enter me

Steady hips and an aggressive pulse
The sound of your skin smacking me
My body is yours; I relinquish control
Take me to a euphoric fantasy

Chest to chest and eye to eye
Reaching higher levels of emotionality
Your rhythm slows down, and I feel you arrive
You take a moment to feel all that's inside of me

The intensity fades, but the passion remains
We both settle back into reality
You hold me tight and stare into my eyes
Have we hit a new peak in our sexuality?

THE SECRET

I won't tell if you won't
Let's keep this entanglement afloat
Our forbidden late-night rendezvous
Would be devastating to expose

We play our parts so no one knows
It's a different story behind closed doors
Alone, we can't keep our hands off each other
The sexual attraction is impossible to ignore

Immoral judgment that satisfies
Fully aware of what we're doing
Acting on impulse, but what's the cost?
Is the risk worth what we could be losing?

An internal battle we need to face
But it's hard for us to stop
I try to compartmentalize our lustful state
As I wait for the other shoe to drop

We understand this needs to end
Or we'll find ourselves with regret
As we lie there in comfortable silence
Holding on to our little secret

KING

I gave this man the best of me
And he couldn't get enough of me
Devoured by his sexual company
It's like the universe was rewarding me

Blown away by how he pleased me
His rapture was to need me
Almost climaxed from the way he teased me
Overcome by how satisfied he'd leave me

I'd never enjoyed this type of magnetism
I told him what I wanted, and he did more than listen
Pleasing my body became his only mission
This fantasy of a man became my new addiction

From my place to his house
Even public spaces
When he wanted me, he had me
It didn't matter where the place is

He woke me from a nightmare
And I only wanted more
Well-versed in his lesson
He inspired me to explore

He laid into my thighs
Until I couldn't take it anymore
He showed me what real sex was like
Not that mediocre shit I used to settle for

I gave this man the best of me
Because he brought me back to life
He showed me how it feels to be properly desired
He brought my sexuality back to light

I cherish our experience together
A piece of him will always be mine
He reawakened my sexual confidence
And divine men like that are hard to find

EVENING

When I'm not with you, I'm daydreaming
Knowing our playtime starts in the evening
As the sun sets, I get that feeling
Anticipation has me fiending

Just waiting for the evening
Thoughts about you have me creaming
My blood is pumping, heavy breathing
I can't wait to spend all night screaming

I text you that I'm leaving
I'm in the car, anxiously speeding
You send me voice notes to start the teasing
Even apart, you know how to please me

My adrenaline is quickly increasing
As the distance between us is easing
We meet at the door, both hearts beating
You pull me in so we can start our evening

PURPOSE

You came into my life for a purpose
Although it was not on purpose

At the time, I felt imperfect
Healing but emotionally malnourished

My history didn't concern us
But after meeting you, my past no longer resurfaced

First impression, it made me feel nervous
Our connection was deeper than surface

An energy that intensely immersed us
Our souls spoke like the universe heard us

Was it fate that was trying to serve us?
I believe that we met for a purpose

MY DARKNESS

If you want to be a part of my light
You have to understand my darkness
What I've been through and how it changed me
Understand the effects of its harshness

You're inspired by the energy I ignite
Recognize that it sparked from my darkness
A light that came out of the shadows
Proof that not all of me is harmless

There's a girl in me who had to fight
Fight my way out of the darkness
I'm now a woman of power and strength
My natural forces I learned to harness

My future is burning bright
And no one can interfere with my progress
If you want to be a part of my light
You have to accept my darkness

PUSHED

You pushed me away
Into someone else's arms
I needed that push
So I could feel love without harm

You pushed me to feel
The unconditional love of a real man
I was conditioned to your false self
In his arms, I now understand

You pushed me, and I let go
Of you and what we shared
It wasn't real, it wasn't love
My sense of judgment has been repaired

You pushed me to self-evaluate
Through pain came self-discovery
I've been energetically recharged
Healing has uncovered me

You pushed me toward awareness
Of myself and those I hold close
Exposed everything, good and bad
I accepted what serves me the most

You pushed me to finally learn
How toxic people can be
How they manipulate your trust
How they drain you spiritually

You pushed me to appreciate
Those who truly love me
The ones who support and honor me
The ones who would never hurt me

You pushed me far away
And with the distance, I've grown
I've embodied my spiritual self
I've reached an empowerment I've never known

PERFECT LOVE

All I want is a perfect love
Is that asking for too much?
The kind of love that overwhelms your mind
The kind of love that makes your blood rush

A perfect love that bonds souls
A connection deeper than surface
Magnetizing your spiritual intention
I want the love that gives your life purpose

The kind of love that inspires greatness
Brings you closer than physical touch
Perfection is a lot to ask for
But I'm not asking for too much

WORTH

I've come up for air
Embodying a rebirth
You quickly entered my life
And I can't help but question your worth

Is it worth taking a risk?
You asked my expectations of you
Are your intentions long-term?
Is it worth falling for you?

I need to know your worth
Because I value my growth
I won't allow another man into my life
Who is inconsistent in his approach

Are you worth my time?
Are you worth the effort?
Are you worth being vulnerable to?
What if I ultimately get hurt?

Only time will tell
And actions will secure
Am I strong enough to let my guard down?
Is it worth it? . . . I'm still unsure

READY

You met me at a unique time
When my heart no longer felt heavy
I was happy, confident, and back to myself
I fully embodied my sexy

Our connection was instant
We were drawn to each other intensely
You listened to my words, my body language
You received my energy intently

You were the creative soul I desired
I was overwhelmed by the vibes you sent me
Sometimes you seemed too good to be true
I wondered if the universe was trying to test me

You wanted more than I could give you
You wanted us to go steady
But I needed time to focus on myself
To be in a relationship—I just wasn't ready

I was back to loving myself
I was focused on me directly
I wanted this time to nurture my spirit
And that affected us, consequently

You respected my boundaries like a man
You showed compassion and love for me, plenty
Thank you for understanding and sticking by my side
I'll come back to you when I'm ready

PERSONAL SPACE

Your love is what I prayed for
But your love is hard to take
You ambush me with affection
Sometimes you tend to suffocate

Unaware of your own tendencies
You're innocent at your core
But too much of a good thing has me
Pulling away versus wanting more

I find comfort in isolation
My time alone is a necessity
To recharge my emotional battery
To grow our relationship in harmony

A confusing conflict of interest
My head and heart are at war
How can I need space
When this is everything I asked for?

Trying to find balance
The resolution depends on me
Prioritizing myself
Without neglecting your needs

To encourage your affection
To not make my anxiety worse
To protect our relationship
I need to put myself first

I want to cater to your emotions
Make our home a safe place
To you, I'll naturally grow closer
If I take some personal space

DECIDE

I don't mean to keep you guessing
But I'm still trying to decide
Decide if you complement my spirit
Decide if I want you by my side

My past relationships have not been easy
This time, I want to consciously try
To avoid choosing another wrong man
This time, I need to choose a good guy

You seem to have it all
I'm confident about what you'll provide
But it's scary for me to trust my heart
Which is why I'm taking time to decide

I'm dating with intent
Taking my uncertainties in stride
To you, it might feel confusing
To me, it feels aligned

I don't want to rush my feelings
Letting my guard down will take some time
I'm thankful for your patience
While I take this time to decide

RELATIONSHIPS

A relationship should not be hurtful
A relationship should not be vain
A relationship should not control you
A relationship should not cause pain

When you consider a relationship
Don't reconsider your wants and needs
Finding yourself in an unhappy trap
Will help you figure out what real love means

If your relationship is hurting you
That's a clear sign to get out
Don't condition yourself to one-sided love
Don't lose yourself on someone else's account

The relationship worth fighting for
Is the one you have with yourself
How you choose to love your entirety
Sets a standard for others as well

LUCKY

People say I'm lucky
It's hard to disagree
I have my health
My wealth
My family
And a positive outlook on life mentally

People will see what they want to see
Assume it comes with no difficulty
Having luck on my side
Didn't come without cost
Because I certainly paid a fee

This luxury, in summary
Is a victory
In my mid-thirties
I take it as a reward
For my self-discovery

I'm focused on me
I'm mindful of my recovery
The more I love myself
The more good things will happen to me

Self-love is the key
Ridding my life of toxic energy
When I embody positivity
The real luck starts with me

BEST LIFE

I'm on my way to my best life
An intuition not yet shown
I get tingles of energy for the future
I know there's only good waiting in the unknown

I feel that I have a higher purpose
That my life hasn't reached its milestone
I trust the signs that encourage my path
A path to the best life that I will soon own

VIBE

It's time to raise my vibe
I've learned to trust the signs
Everything will turn out right
Because I trust in the divine

I have prosperity on my mind
I know luck is on my side
My future unfolds by my design
As long as I'm living on a higher vibe

LOVE SONG

Laughter is my new love song
Its melody brings me peace
The feel-good tingles on my skin
I'm vibing to chuckle beats

This spontaneity of joyful sound
Is my happiness increased
It's pure, it's calm, it's genuine
It's an embodiment of me

A song I want to share with the world
And play it on repeat
I'm happy, I'm positive, I'm centered
I don't want my love song to ever cease

CHERISH

Cherish the good days
Waking up feeling thankful for it all
You look at your life
No negative lessons to recall

Cherish the good things
Open your spirit to receive it all
Get drunk on self-love
Don't go through withdrawal

Cherish the good life
Every blessing big and small
When you have love, health, and peace of mind
You'll realize you have it all

WHAT I'VE LEARNED

I've learned happiness starts with me

I've learned manifestation should be in my daily routine

I've learned to trust the universe and let the divine intervene

I've learned self-love is the only path to recovery

I've learned success is what I believe it to be

I've learned putting myself first does not require an apology

I've learned spiritual solitude gives me clarity

I've learned failure does not define me

I've learned to reflect on my insecurities

I've learned I'm not alone on my journey

I've learned forgiveness is a form of therapy

I've learned the importance of trust and loyalty

I've learned to spread positivity

I've learned to be thankful for the beautiful things given to me

I've learned to rejoice in my serenity

I've learned laughter can be life's melody

I've learned the future holds no guarantee

I've learned to radiate my inner beauty

I've learned healthier habits regarding what I put in my body

I've learned the influence a smile can have on society

I've learned the value of time when you're living intently

I've learned I'm responsible for everything I achieve

I've learned to stay true to what I believe

I've learned to value every moment spent with my family

I've learned how to stay motivated on the path to my dream

I've learned all these lessons by simply loving me

LET LOVE BE

Let love be new
Let love be kind
Let it come correctly
Don't let love become blind

Let love be honest
Let love be divine
Let it be vulnerable
Let love come in good time

ACKNOWLEDGMENTS

This book is a testament to the power of transformation and healing. It was written in the depths of heartbreak, when the weight of a toxic relationship had left me feeling fractured and lost. Each poem serves as a small step toward reclaiming myself—a cathartic release of pain, confusion, and the ghosts of my past. Writing became my therapy, my safe space to unravel the broken pieces of who I once was and, in time, piece them back together. The pages of this book are where I found my voice, where I shed old versions of myself, and where I learned how to love the person I was becoming. It was through these words that I began to reinvent my life, embracing the journey of self-discovery and self-love.

And while this journey has been mine, it has also been shaped by the incredible people who have walked alongside me. To everyone who has supported me, cheered me on, and listened when I needed to be heard—thank you. Whether through quiet encouragement or by simply being a witness to my growth, your presence has meant more than you know.

A special thank you to my fiancé, Adam, whose unwavering belief was the spark that finally lit the fire to get this book published.

Most of all, I am forever grateful to myself—for showing up every day and choosing healing over staying stuck, for daring to release the past in order to create the future I deserve. This book is not just a reflection of who I was; it is a celebration of who I have become.

To the person I was when I started this journey: thank you for surviving.
To the person I am now: I love you, and I am proud of you.
To the ones who hurt me: thank you for teaching me my worth, even in your absence.

Finally, to the readers who will find themselves within these pages: if these words reach you and make you feel understood, then this book has fulfilled its purpose. This collection is dedicated to those who have loved deeply and who have been hurt yet found the courage to rise from the ashes. May you know that healing is a journey, and even in our most fragile moments, we are capable of rediscovering our strength. I am living proof that we can heal, we can reinvent ourselves, and we can love ourselves again.

With endless love and gratitude,
Amanda

www.ingramcontent.com/pod-product-compliance
Lightning Source LLC
Chambersburg PA
CBHW021138130626
46554CB00005B/1559